S_...

you want to find out more
about following Jesus?

That's terrific!

Following Jesus is great

So let's get going…

You've probably played 'Follow the Leader' many times, so you already know that to follow someone means that they are leading the way.

Following Jesus means *he* is the leader.

This is what Jesus' first followers did. They called him 'Master' and 'Lord': names which mean 'You are our leader'.

(You can look at this in the Bible in the book of Mark, chapter 1 verses 16 to 20)

Didn't Jesus die about 2000 years ago?

Yes. He was put to death on a cross in Jerusalem around 30 AD.

You can read about Jesus' death in Luke chapter 23.

But three days later he came alive again. Now he lives in heaven. Since he is alive, though we cannot see him, we can talk to him and ask him to be our leader today.

This is an amazing claim. Let's look at the facts to check out if it is true.

Jesus' tomb was empty.

Many of Jesus' first followers saw him alive again. *Not once, but several times.*

You can read a short list of some of Jesus' appearances after he rose again in 1 Corinthians chapter 15 verses 3 to 8. You can read some of these stories in full in Luke chapter 24.

Jesus had promised to send his followers a helper, the Holy Spirit. After receiving the Holy Spirit these followers changed…

…from people who were scared stiff…

…into people who were not afraid to say they were followers of Jesus.

You can read about the changes in Jesus' followers in Acts, chapters 1 to 3.

Millions of people ever since have found their lives changed as they have asked Jesus to be their leader.

We believe that the best explanation of the facts is that Jesus really did rise again: he is alive today and we can follow him.

Okay, so Jesus rose again and he is alive now.

But I like being in charge of my own life. I'm not sure I want him to be my leader.

I'm not sure I want Jesus to be my leader

This is something we all think and feel. But is it the best way for us to live?

Everyone of us is made by God. As our Maker he knows the best way for us to live. That way is the way of love, goodness and justice.

(You can read about God being our Maker in Psalm 139)

But all of us have chosen to follow our own way rather than God's. This leads to us being selfish, unkind, greedy and rude. We may not be like this all of the time, but all of us do live like this some of the time.

(You can read about this in Romans, chapter 3 verses 10 and 11)

Yet even though we have turned our backs on God's way, he still loves us.

He wants to forgive us and help us. That is why Jesus came.

In his life Jesus showed us and told us what living God's way all the time was like.

Then he died as the means by which all our wrong thoughts, words and deeds could be forgiven. This means we can be put back on God's way rather than our own.

You can read about this in 1 John chapter 1 verses 8 to 10.

So now let's go back to how we can begin to follow Jesus today.

We need to say something like:

When we ask God to forgive us and accept us as one of Jesus' followers, he always says **'yes'**.

From that moment Jesus is our Leader and God's Holy Spirit has come to live in us and help us be good followers.

You can check this out in 1 John chapter 5 verses 11 to 15.

Keep on following

God has given us some things to help us to be good followers of Jesus.

Listen to the leader

The Bible is especially important here. As we read it we find out more about God's way and so know more of what he wants us to do.

Talk to the leader

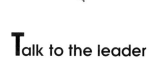

We can talk to Jesus any time, anywhere and about anything. We do not have to use any special words. We can do this on our own and when we are with other followers of Jesus.

Do what the leader says

When it is clear what Jesus wants us to do, then we should always do it.